What Our Readers Have Said...

"Although I consider myself a seasoned sales professional, it is helpful to have past learning's refreshed. The books were also beneficial because of the information concerning 'trends' in the sales relationship. The sales process should be viewed as dynamic since business relationships change regularly."

•

"For the particular business I am in and the type of sales calls I have, I find that the books in the Pinpoint Sales Training Series are very often applicable to how I conduct business. I would recommend them to other sales people, just not ones that are in my industry."

•

"These books provide very good concepts. It fits in well with the Bell Leadership training program that I attended in November."

•

"I use this material in these books and apply it to my customers and other employees I work with."

•

"I would like to know other topics. Is there anything on Production Management or Consultative Selling or Time Management?"

•

"These books are great tools that should be used as guidelines for our everyday

supervisory practices. You need to take the time to do a short self-evaluation when reading them."

•

"The Pinpoint Training Series delivers information that could be used in a lot different areas."

•

"I like this because I can take them with me to read at a convenient time. I feel the little time I have to spend in the office is best use on activities that directly relate to revenue opportunities. I like the short amount of time it takes to keep up with these."

•

"I prefer the self-study approach; it fits in with my schedule."

•

"My thought is that the real value of these books comes into effect when doing the action plans."

•

"Short and sweet. These books are easy to comprehend."

•

"I have enjoyed reading these books. They are relevant to today's work environment and the ongoing change in the way we manage our workforce."

•

"I do feel that these books have been very helpful to me at my job."

•

"I think a lot of the recommendations in these books are very useful, and can be applicable to everyday situations. If nothing else, it's a good reference guide to fall back upon if a situation arises in the future."

•

"These books are relevant to today's work environment and the ongoing change in the way we manage our workforce."

•

Strengthening Customer Retention

Pinpoint Sales Skill Development Training Series

TIMOTHY F. BEDNARZ

MAJORIUM
BUSINESS PRESS

Pinpoint Sales Skill Development Training Series
"Strengthening Customer Retention"
Timothy F. Bednarz

Graphic design: Monika Pawlak

Majorium Business Press
2025 Main Street
Stevens Point, WI 54481
715.342.1018 • 800.654.4935

ISBN 978-1-882181-85-8

Printed in the United States of America

Introduction

The Pinpoint Sales Skill Development Training Series is designed for targeted training and education regarding increased improvement in a specific skill or competency.

Each book within this series is designed to be easy to use, understand and apply to your job. It can be used as a basis for training individuals, as a discussion guide or as a personal training tool.

Each chapter within this book discusses a specific concept. When you have completed all eight chapters you should have a 360° perspective of the topic.

Additionally, each chapter is divided into specific sections:

- The first section provides you with an overview of the topic

- The Implications section discusses why the concept is important, and why it is important to learn and apply.

- The Strategies, Tips & Techniques to Apply section teaches how to use and apply the particular concept to your work.

- The Points to Ponder section gives you something to think about or to be discussed with a group setting. These are questions not meant to be immediately answered, but to be pondered over time.

- The Training Activity section provides you with the tools to transfer what you have learned to your job. It is designed to help create an action plan to effectively apply the concept.

Each of the topics in this series is time-tested and proven in the market-place. They have been used by thousands of employees as training tools. Many of the users have commented that what made these books valuable, was the ability to refer to them when a problem surfaced. They indicated that they remembered reading about the exact problem. They referred back to these books and found an appropriate solution.

You will find them equally valuable as a resource in your professional development library.

Table of Contents

LEARNING OBJECTIVES:

- The importance of customer retention.
- To analyze customer retention strategies and how they affect their sales.
- To apply techniques to increase customer retention.
- To monitor customer retention.

1

Understanding Customer Retention

When the economy softens and turns sour, companies rush to downsize, reduce budgets and slash the size of their organization. Yet research has demonstrated that this is the wrong approach to take. Rather than reduce operating budgets, companies can achieve the same goal by increasing customer retention.

▓ IMPLICATIONS — WHAT THIS MEANS TO YOU

Most companies accept a 20% turnover in customers as normal. Companies close, move and change suppliers. However, research performed by the Harvard Business School demonstrated that if companies can reduce this number to 15% and retain an additional 5% of their customers, they will impact their profitability equivalent to a 10% reduction in their operating budget.

Salespeople have the power and control to build and nurture customer relationships. Their personal actions and activities with individual customers can determine the future of the relationship. Most salespeople underestimate the impact that they can have on the success and profitability of their companies.

▓ STRATEGIES, TIPS & TECHNIQUES TO APPLY

Several critical factors form the foundation of every customer relationship and customer retention. These include:

Value

Although salespeople often cite price as a primary reason why prospects and customers buy a product or service, they are wrong. Buyers are not as concerned with the price or cost of a product as they are with the value they are receiving. Value is defined as regularly meeting or exceeding a customer's expectations. These can include their expectations of a product or service, salesperson, service or the vendor. The salesperson who can consistently deliver value is undoubtedly able to increase their customer retention rate.

The customer's overall perception of the value received is the number one determining factor in whether the customer remains or switches to a competitor.

Trust

Every time a prospect or customer places an order they are making a leap of faith, ultimately trusting what was said and represented by the salesperson. As salespeople stand behind their words, the bond of trust deepens. The deeper the bond, the harder it will be for the customer to switch to another supplier.

If salespeople think that the concepts of trust and integrity have become passé in recent years, they should look at the impact of the collapse of companies like Enron, Arthur Andersen, and WorldCom and the ramifications on their customer and investor base once it became evident that they severed the relationship of trust.

Arthur Andersen, once their credibility was severely damaged, experienced a wholesale abandonment of both customers and key employees in a very short time, leaving a shell of what was once a major corporation. Long-time customers quickly found a competitor to take Andersen's place.

Credibility

Long-term customer relationships are facilitated by credibility. A salesperson builds his or her credibility in several ways. Obviously, without trust salespeople will have no personal credibility, and what they say or do will not be believed by the customer. However, credibility is also defined by the experience and expertise that each salesperson brings to the customer. The salesperson's personal experience and expertise is the differentiating factor in most sales and what delivers value. This is because an experienced salesperson can apply his or her expertise to craft unique solutions for the customer that solve existing problems and lay nagging concerns to rest. Without the personal experience and expertise, these solutions are not credible.

Reliability

An additional aspect of value is the reliability of the products or services being purchased by customers. They want products and services to perform in a consistent and dependable fashion. Customers are trusting salespeople to deliver solutions that can be relied upon to resolve a problem and improve overall performance.

On another level, customers expect salespeople to be reliable in both their words and actions. They want salespeople to be available when needed and counted on to look out for their interests.

Responsiveness

Customers expect both salespeople and the companies they represent to be responsive to their needs, especially when a problem arises. Most customers are pragmatic and understand that problems and glitches will occur as a normal part of any business operation. However, they also expect salespeople and their companies to react quickly to fix the problem to their satisfaction in a fair and consistent manner.

Problems are moments of truth in the customer relationship. The angriest customer can be converted into an advocate with quick resolution to a problem. The reverse is also true: when salespeople and companies are unresponsive to a customer's needs and problems and cause undue hardship, they can quickly turn a customer into an activist who will take the time and effort to damage the salesperson and his or her company's reputation.

Empathy

Everyone wants to feel important. Customers want to know that their business is valued and important to the salesperson. They do not want to be taken advantage of or be taken for granted.

Customer retention demands the active participation of the salesperson to foster and nurture the relationship so that the customer knows that their business is valued, no matter how big or small their account is.

POINTS TO PONDER — SOMETHING TO THINK ABOUT

1. Do you value your customer's business or view them as a means to make money?
2. How important is developing relationships with customers to you?

TRAINING ACTIVITY — APPLICATION & ACTION PLAN

Define the ways that you deliver value to your customers.

1. Identify who you regularly meet or exceed your customer's expectations
2. Identify how you build and sustain trust and credibility.
3. How do you show your customers that they are valued and important to you?
4. Pinpoint areas of weakness that need to be improved.

2

The Factors
Affecting Customer Retention

C ustomer retention does not occur through happenstance. Successful retention is planned and carefully implemented. Salespeople must take the time and effort to both manage and nurture their existing accounts if they wish to increase their rates of overall retention.

▓ IMPLICATIONS — WHAT THIS MEANS TO YOU

Many salespeople believe that they should spend the majority of their time developing new sales and business. However, survey after survey has shown that the best source of new business is often an existing customer.

If salespeople pay careful attention to account development and retention they will see their overall results increase. Rather than devote the majority of their time to new business development, salespeople should use a balanced approach that allows them to spend an equal or greater amount of time on expanding the business in their existing accounts.

▓ STRATEGIES, TIPS & TECHNIQUES TO APPLY

There are a number of factors that impact customer retention that salespeople should be aware of and should take care to manage if they wish to increase both customer loyalty and satisfaction. These include:

Experience

The salesperson has the ability and the responsibility to manage the customer's experience. Some companies use the "Circle of Service" concept to plot and plan every step of the customer's experience with their company, leaving nothing to chance and insuring a positive customer experience.

The salesperson initiates the overall customer experience when he or she starts the sales process, and it continues until the customer ceases to do business with the salesperson's company. It includes every aspect of the business relationship and is defined by every contact the customer has with the salesperson or with a representative of his or her company. It is also defined by ease of product use and how easy it is to work with the salesperson and their company to resolve problems or complaints, fulfill additional orders and a host of other issues that may arise in the course of the relationship.

Salespeople have the ability to successfully manage the customer experience by anticipating needs and problems, by informing the customer how to handle specific situations, and by being actively available to meet the customer's needs. This is enhanced by a service mentality to work to meet the customer's wants and needs.

Quality

The overall quality of the product or service is often a determining factor in customer retention. Products that perform flawlessly, up to specification and as promised increase customer satisfaction. When products are flawed or produce problems and production failures or shutdowns, customers will be prone to look for a more reliable vendor.

Often initial problems that are sources of heightened frustration are due to poor customer training and education. Unfamiliar with the use and application of a new product or service, many problems can, and often do occur. Salespeople can anticipate these initial problems and reduce customer frustrations by making sure that all end-users are trained and educated in the use of the new products or services. This should include the use and application of all advanced features. Users often know how to use the basic features of a product or service but are never taught how to maximize its performance. These are the areas that salespeople emphasize and sell, but often customers never realize the full benefits due to poor training and education.

Satisfaction

There is a strong correlation between customer satisfaction and loyalty. The higher the levels of satisfaction, the more intensely loyal customers are.

When salespeople pay attention to all of the details involved in a relationship with a customer and carefully manage their experience, they assure satisfaction. However, satisfaction is fragile, and can quickly fade if not properly managed.

It should be noted that the shaping of perceptions and customer expectations during the sales process plays a critical role in customer satisfaction. Carefully managed and shaped expectations will result in a satisfied customer. If the salesperson failed to identify and manage the customer's expectations, or overhyped his or her product or service, problems will arise. Companies can deliver exactly what was promised, but still fail to meet a customer's expectations. Thus salespeople should carefully define the customer's expectations at the time of the order and make sure that they are realistic, otherwise they can expect problems to develop later on after the product or service is delivered.

Valued

Customers expect that they will not be taken for granted. Each wants to know that their business is important and valued by the salesperson and his or her company. If the customer senses that they are not valued or are being taken advantage of they will look for a new supplier.

Value

The customer's perceived value of the product they purchased is the bottom line in customer retention. Salespeople should note that this perception will vary from customer to customer. As a rule of thumb, value is defined as meeting or exceeding the customer's expectations on a regular basis. Since perceptions and expectations vary by individual and are impacted by previous experiences with other companies and suppliers, this can be a difficult thing to manage. However, the salesperson who does take the time to make sure they deliver value to their customers will be at an advantage, because the competition generally does not.

POINTS TO PONDER — SOMETHING TO THINK ABOUT

1. Are there any other factors you think are important to consider in the effort to retain your customers?

2. Have you lost business because of a failure to pay attention to these factors?

TRAINING ACTIVITY — APPLICATION & ACTION PLAN

Select your five top customers and analyze the business opportunities that they represent.

1. Ascertain whether there are plans for new products or product lines.

2. Determine if there are plans for acquisitions or mergers.

3. Identify areas in which you can but are not currently selling your products or services.

4. Develop strategies to expand your business in these accounts.

3

Indifference Makes Customers Walk

Many salespeople will sell a prospect, get the order, and walk away. They may check up to make sure the order has been received and the customer is happy with it and then move on to more pressing matters. If the customer orders frequently, the salesperson may be in contact on a regular basis, but what should the salesperson do when he or she sells products that have long cycles between orders? This is the time when competitors can make real inroads into the account without the salesperson's knowledge.

▨ IMPLICATIONS — WHAT THIS MEANS TO YOU

Many salespeople assume that since they haven't heard anything, their customer is happy, yet only 4% of unhappy customers are vocal about their problems. An astonishing 96% of unhappy customers quietly take their business elsewhere. If the salesperson never calls to check on them, their decision to switch suppliers has been validated.

From a psychological perspective, customers want to know that their business is not only important but also highly valued by the salesperson. When salespeople only call when it's time to reorder, the customer develops a sense that they are being taken advantage of and being used by the salesperson to get a commission check.

Every business is affected and impacted by the forces of technology and the global economy. Businesses are transforming themselves at an increasingly rapid rate to adapt to an even faster pace of change, which means customer needs are changing just as quickly. This translates into new opportunities that are readily missed if the salesperson doesn't take the time to follow up and examine their clients' needs on a regular basis.

There are additional benefits to regularly calling upon existing customers. Small accounts can turn into major accounts overnight for a variety of reasons, including expansion or the positioning of new facilities at an existing location. Unless salespeople take the time to stay informed, they may "miss the boat" and see the opportunity pass to a competitor.

The salesperson who is not attuned to the needs of their customers or interested in building long-term relationships has positioned him or herself at a real competitive disadvantage.

The salesperson may assume the customer's business will always be there, but may be in for a shock when the competition takes the business out from under them.

At a time when customer retention is critical to most businesses, it is an excellent idea for salespeople to add customer checkup calls to their to-do list. Salespeople should make it a habit to regularly and periodically go down their customer list and call to make sure each is satisfied and to identify any potential needs or opportunities that demand immediate attention.

As they place these calls, salespeople should explain to the customer that they understand it will be a while before the customer will be ordering again, but they just want to ensure that everything is going smoothly.

If problems are identified, salespeople should take the time to solve them. Problems or not, salespeople will find that a periodic call will be appreciated. This reassures the customer that they are valued and important and reemphasizes customer satisfaction.

It is often not only what a salesperson does that counts, but also what other salespeople fail to do. Checking up on customers on a regular basis is one small but very effective way to differentiate themselves from the competition.

TRAINING ACTIVITY — APPLICATION & ACTION PLAN

1. Identify any customers lost due to indifference or an assumption they were loyal to you.
2. Identify what happened.
3. Determine what could you have done differently.
4. Based upon your analysis, identify the strategies you need to employ to keep in touch with your customers to assure their expectations are met and they are happy with your product or service.

4

Customers at Risk

Salespeople can never assume their business is completely safe. Major accounts are always at risk, and even more so during times of economic uncertainty. Competition intensifies when companies struggle to grasp the economic realities of recessionary and post-recessionary markets where uncertainty prevails.

IMPLICATIONS — WHAT THIS MEANS TO YOU

Unstable economic conditions heavily impact most salespeople. Many, especially in the capital goods sector, have continued to experience a sluggish return to past sales levels.

The pressure placed on them by their sales managers to produce in the face of continual sagging market conditions intensifies the stress experienced by salespeople during an economic downturn. All companies are under pressure to reinforce and stabilize their customer base. Volatile market conditions render the competition extremely dangerous, as many struggle to survive.

Salespeople must develop proactive sales strategies to protect existing business while exploring new markets for additional business to replace the losses experienced during an economic downturn. As competition continues to heat up in the struggle for market share, salespeople cannot become complacent about protecting the business base they have already established.

Salespeople cannot afford to sit back and hope for the best. They must be aggressive in identifying their at-risk customers and prospects. Once they have done this, they need to identify the actions that need to be taken to protect these precarious accounts. Salespeople can use the following strategies to buttress an existing account or recover one about to be lost.

Identify the Risk Factors

The initial step for salespeople to take is to identify the risk factors that are affecting a specific customer. This includes confirming that the customer is actually at risk, and not just a victim of slowing market conditions. Salespeople may need to confirm that the customer indeed is being courted by a competitor and in the process of evaluating their products and services.

Confirm the Risk

Once salespeople have identified with some degree of certainty that their customer is at risk, they need to meet with the buyer to confirm that he or she is considering a competitor's offer.

At this point it is not wise for salespeople to confront the buyer. Rather, they should gingerly approach the subject and ask them to confirm whether they are considering a competitor's products or services.

Determine the Level of Risk

Once the buyer has confirmed that they are considering other products and services, the salesperson will need to probe further to determine the actual level of risk. This includes identifying how far into the evaluation process the customer has proceeded and the results of his or her evaluation.

Salespeople also need to probe for additional information as to how well the buyer likes the competitor's products and what is specifically liked or disliked regarding them. This information will provide the basis for a counteroffer. Salespeople will also need to determine the price and other pertinent information if the buyer is willing to share it with them.

Identify the Problems and Issues

It is essential for salespeople to probe to determine what prompted the buyer to consider the competition. They need to identify whether there was a specific problem with their product and determine what the competition is offering that they can't provide.

The customer is obviously dissatisfied with something to open the doors to the competition. Their business cannot be recovered until these problems and issues are brought into the open and resolved.

Identify Potential Solutions

Once salespeople have collected answers to these four areas listed above, they can craft a series of potential solutions for the customer. If there is a strong relationship and rapport with the buyer, it is likely that the salesperson's proposal will be carefully considered.

Gain Acceptance

If the buyer is open to the salesperson's solutions and recommendations, it is time to resell them on the reasons why they bought in the first place. The salesperson must use the good will developed over the term of the relationship to remind and resell the buyer on the benefits of continuing the sales relationship.

Seek Commitment

The final step is to resell the buyer and seek a commitment to remaining with the salesperson and his or her company. During this process, new products and technologies may have to be introduced or pricing renegotiated. The buyer should see that the salesperson is willing to take the necessary steps to keep their business, solve their problems and support their goals and objectives.

Salespeople need to trade on the value of their relationship with their customer. Unless a major problem has occurred that broke the trust, salespeople should have the inside track over a new competitor. Now is the time to "pull out all the stops" to make sure the customer remains with them.

TRAINING ACTIVITY — APPLICATION & ACTION PLAN

1. Identify a potential customer who you feel may be at risk.

2. Develop a sales strategy to recover and reconfirm their commitment to you using the strategy listed above.

5

Paying Attention to Your Customers Is Good Business

When a sale is lost, it's often blamed on the competition and the fact that they came in with a better price or superior product. Yet according to a Forum Corporation survey, the number one reason customers stop buying is poor service or lack of attention (65%), with lower price (15%) and a better product (15%) by far secondary causes.

IMPLICATIONS — WHAT THIS MEANS TO YOU

The impact of good service—and increased customer retention—on the individual salesperson can be dramatic. By increasing the level of customer service and support, salespeople are able to stabilize their sales base and commissions. New orders will expand the salesperson's base rather than merely replace lost commissions. When compounded over several years, a salesperson will experience an overall increase in their sales income.

The second impact of good service is the expansion of existing business. Salespeople often fail to look at their existing customers as the easiest place to develop new business. They fail to pursue additional opportunities with happy customers. These additional opportunities for new and expanded business become readily apparent to salespeople as they concentrate their time and effort on servicing a current customer.

The bottom line for salespeople is that paying attention to the customer is critical to their existing business and commission base.

According to a Harvard School of Business survey, customer retention is profitable. The old rule of thumb was all businesses lose 10% of their customer base every year. Harvard discovered that the retention of 2% of the 10% annual loss is comparable to a 10% increase in bottom-line profitability. Consequently, good customer service techniques focused on customer retention are profitable to both the individual salesperson and their company.

These retention techniques include:

Visibility

The greatest fear voiced by many customers is that the salesperson will disappear immediately after the sale. Salespeople can minimize these fears by focusing on the needs and expectations of the customer. Salespeople must fully recognize that from the customer's perspective the sale begins once the order has been placed. Anything up to that point was merely part of the decision making process.

Salespeople need to be highly visible immediately after the sale, during the delivery, installation and training phases of the order. They cannot afford to leave anything to chance. Attention to detail every step of the way will reap the salesperson tremendous dividends in professional reputation and customer retention through increased customer satisfaction.

Continual Education

As a product expert, salespeople should continually revisit the customer to ensure they are taking advantage of all features the product or service can deliver. Salespeople often emphasize these during their sales presentations, but many customer fail to achieve the full level of satisfaction because they are not fully trained and educated in how to maximize the use and application of a product or service.

Thus it is in the salesperson's best interest to educate his or her customers as to the best use and application of their products or services. This knowledge often "falls through the cracks" because various individuals assume that it is the responsibility of another employee to fully train and educate the customer.

Salespeople must ensure the customer's investment in their product has been maximized. They must make sure the value they have promised during the sale has been delivered and fully acknowledged by the customer.

Minimize Problems and Frustrations

Salespeople who frequently and regularly visit their customers can minimize minor problems and nagging frustrations that are often the cause of lost business. It is not sufficient to simply talk with a buyer or decision maker. Salespeople must spend time with the end-user who is personally experiencing these problems, as their feedback and input influences the decision maker, who can then identify any sources of pain to a competitive salesperson.

The best defense salespeople can launch against the competition is to continually interact with these individuals and to keep them happy. They are in the best position to help the salesperson prevent the competition from gaining a foothold in the account.

> ## POINTS TO PONDER — SOMETHING TO THINK ABOUT
>
> 1. What has been your typical post-sale attitude toward your customers?
> 2. When do you consider your job and responsibility to the customer over?

TRAINING ACTIVITY — APPLICATION & ACTION PLAN

Conduct an analysis of your post-sale activities:

1. Determine how you treat the customer once the sale is made.

2. Identify ways to improve your follow-up activities.

3. Pinpoint ways you can increase your visibility for new and existing customers.

4. Identify ways to show your customers you appreciate their business and do not take them for granted.

6

Sewing Up the Customer

Many salespeople have seen a sale completely disintegrate after the customer receives delivery. In shock they ask themselves, "What happened?" Many times such a meltdown is the result of the product or service not meeting the expectations the salesperson has created and sold. While the expectations a salesperson develops may be entirely truthful, someone in the salesperson's company may have "dropped the ball," resulting in the loss of the sale. In either case the salesperson has no doubt lost the customer's long-term business.

IMPLICATIONS — WHAT THIS MEANS TO YOU

Other than the loss of the sale and the resulting commission, this situation also damages the reputation of both the salesperson and their company. In essence, the trust between the salesperson and the customer has been broken, and it will be difficult if not impossible to recover. Lost accounts are often due to the salesperson failing to follow up on the order after it has been delivered. This is the biggest fear most customers have: that the salesperson will forget them after the sale.

STRATEGIES, TIPS & TECHNIQUES TO APPLY

The post-sales loss of a customer is a painful lesson for any salesperson to learn. It has far-reaching consequences not only in regards to the lost customer, but often with the salesperson's manager.

The customer buys because they believe a product or service will help them increase productivity or solve a problem. When the purchase instead leads to additional problems, salespeople are literally thrown out the door. Therefore it is important to make certain the product or service lives up to its promises without creating additional difficulties. The salesperson can maintain control over the entire process and anticipate and minimize problems through effective follow-ups.

After a sale is closed, salespeople need to carefully follow up with the customer to anticipate and surmount potential problems in four critical areas:

Delivery

Salespeople need to ensure that their product will be delivered at the right place and at the right time. They cannot afford to assume anything at this critical stage and should verify they have the right delivery information and the proper contact.

Secondly, salespeople need to continually double-check with their company to ensure that the product is in stock, that any needed modifications were made, and that the product is certain to be delivered on the date promised. In addition, the customer should be immediately informed of any delays and modifications to order processing or delivery.

Salespeople should contact the customer on the shipping date to inform them that the product has been sent, then again to confirm that the product was received on time and in good condition. During this contact discussion, salespeople should seek any input that could disclose a potential problem and listen for comments that verify the customer's overall satisfaction.

Installation

Salespeople should not leave installation to chance by referring the customer to a product manual or website for instructions. They should personalize installation by making sure that someone (ideally the most experienced service person) is actually present for explanations and to be a verbal guide to walk customers through the steps involved. This makes the entire installation procedure and the asking of any questions far easier on the customer.

It is also essential that salespeople are available throughout the installation process. If they are unable to attend, they should make sure to contact the customer in order to verify that he or she is happy with the installation and service. Additionally, salespeople must follow up with the installation person to find out if any problems (major or minor) were experienced or if the customer expressed any concerns.

Training

Proper training of the customer's staff is the only way to ensure that the product or service is being used correctly. Due to inadequate training, customers will often use only the basic features of a product and fail to realize its full potential. Proper training should include a review and demonstration of all product features and benefits. The end-users or operators should be taken step-by-step through each product application.

Invoicing

An incorrect invoice can highly irritate a customer and easily destroys the good will the salesperson has worked hard to develop. As an additional service, salespeople should follow up with the customer to ensure they have been invoiced properly. Salespeople can request that a copy of the invoice be forwarded to them from their accounting department as a personal safeguard.

If a problem does occur, salespeople should take the paperwork directly to the billing department to ensure it is handled properly. They cannot leave anything to chance, and should follow up with the customer to ensure that the invoicing process and procedure was handled satisfactorily.

TRAINING ACTIVITY — APPLICATION & ACTION PLAN

1. Examine ways that you can eliminate barriers to value-added service and increase customer satisfaction in the following areas:

   - Delivery

   - Installation

   - Training

   - Invoicing

2. Identify the biggest problem areas and take steps to eliminate any potential problems for your customers.

7

There Are Many Ways to Lose Business

When considering lost business, one might initially think that it means a major account or bid is lost to a competitor. However, there are many ways that your customer base can be at risk, especially when the economy slows down and sales soften.

IMPLICATIONS — WHAT THIS MEANS TO YOU

Sales books of customers are at a higher risk during economic slowdowns than any other time. If salespeople do not take the time to protect their business, a simple mistake can be extremely costly in terms of lost commissions, lost profits and additional costs to the company.

It costs approximately five times more to get new business than it does to keep existing accounts. It makes eminently more sense for salespeople to take the time and effort to hold on to what they already have than to risk going out into an increasingly competitive economic landscape to search for new business.

STRATEGIES, TIPS & TECHNIQUES TO APPLY

Salespeople need to recognize that all of their business can be at risk during times of economic uncertainty and that there are a number of factors that can affect their book of business.

Uncontrolled Events

Certain events over which salespeople have no control can affect existing business. These can include bankruptcies, plant closings, relocation and layoffs. A major account closing, moving or going bankrupt can have a profound impact on sales. The volume of business can also be greatly reduced if a customer lays off employees and reduces capacity.

While salespeople cannot control the events shaping the future with their customers, they *can* anticipate many of them. As such, they should identify at-risk accounts and stay abreast of the industry changes and trends impacting their customers.

Increased Competition

Competition will intensify during slow economic periods. The available pool of current and potential customers will shrink as market players look to replace lost business. The competition can become increasingly erratic and irrational, with some greatly reducing their prices to buy market share. They will gladly trade dollars for profits just to keep their doors open.

Increased competition can render more sales proposals at risk. Competitors may wage price wars or add considerable incentives to get new business. Thus, in order to position themselves most favorably, it behooves salespeople to develop as much current competitive information as possible including rivals who might be expanding into their market. Many large competitors, who may not have been a factor in the past, are now reaching for smaller customers to help counter their losses.

Reduced Quality and Service

To reduce expenses, a salesperson's own company might make strategic moves affecting the quality of its products or services. Customers directly feeling the impact may become increasingly dissatisfied with the quality of product they are receiving, especially if they are paying more for it.

The effect of any changes in the economy or a salesperson's company is that now is the time to fight for their customers' business. Salespeople should be proactive and keep in touch with their major accounts to ensure that they remain happy with them and their company. Quality and consistency should be maintained at all costs. Action should be taken to rectify any problems the moment they appear, and customers educated about alternatives to the products they are currently buying.

POINTS TO PONDER — SOMETHING TO THINK ABOUT

1. How much of your existing sales base is experiencing problems due to the current economic conditions?

2. Have you been able to identify potential opportunities that have arisen because of the existing economic conditions? Explain.

TRAINING ACTIVITY — APPLICATION & ACTION PLAN

1. Review your existing list of customers. Identify the customers that are at risk due to uncontrollable events, increased competition and/or reduced quality and develop a sales strategy to stabilize the account where possible.

2. For the customers identified to be at risk due to uncontrollable events, identify other sources of potential business to replace these losses.

8

Increasing Customer Retention

It is surprising how many salespeople and companies subconsciously put their customers at risk to be lost to the competition. While many companies experience a certain degree of annual customer turnover due to uncontrollable circumstances, there is a controllable amount of customer turnover that many salespeople and companies surrender to nothing other than poor service attitudes and policies.

IMPLICATIONS — WHAT THIS MEANS TO YOU

Good sales service is an attitude that salespeople must develop if they wish to increase their customer retention rate. Retention levels are a direct reflection of the salesperson's attitude toward and attention to customer problems. Surveys have shown the stronger the response rate and attitude of service, the higher the rate of customer retention.

How salespeople view their customers will determine the degree to which they subject their account base to risk. While good service should be instinctive, some salespeople and companies are indifferent toward and even contemptuous of their accounts. They view problems as caused by ignorant customers rather than by their own failure to properly train and service them.

▦ STRATEGIES, TIPS & TECHNIQUES TO APPLY

A U.S. Office of Consumer Affairs, Technical Assistance Research Institute study revealed patterns in customer behavior as they relate to customer retention.

The following responses were received to the question, "How many of your unhappy customers will buy from you again?"

Minor Complaints

- Non-Complainers – 37%
- Complaints Not Resolved – 46%
- Complaints Resolved – 70%
- Complaints Resolved Quickly – 95%

Major Complaints

- Non-Complainers – 9%
- Complaints Not Resolved – 19%
- Complaints Resolved – 54%
- Complaints Resolved Quickly – 82%

These findings have strong implications for salespeople especially when considered from the perspective of: "How many of your unhappy customers are going to buy from a competitor?"

Minor Complaints

- Non-Complainers – 63%
- Complaints Not Resolved – 54%
- Complaints Resolved – 30%
- Complaints Resolved Quickly – 5%

Major Complaints

- Non-Complainers – 91%

- Complaints Not Resolved – 81%
- Complaints Resolved – 46%
- Complaints Resolved Quickly – 18%

These findings—and the high potential for a competitor to take business once a problem occurs—should be a wake-up call for any salesperson interested in building their base and retaining business. The above findings specifically indicate that:

Salespeople Must Pay Attention to Their Customers

The biggest threat to salespeople lies in hidden problems they are unaware of. Much akin to a farmer failing to tend his fields, when salespeople fail to tend to their existing customer base and unbeknownst to them a problem arises, there is a 63 to 91% possibility of losing the customer. While the likelihood of a major problem existing in the first place tempers these numbers, problems of varying degrees will always arise. Even a minor problem causing a nagging frustration to a customer elevates the risk of them going to the competition.

Rather than passively tending their customers, salespeople must be proactive in their approach. They must openly communicate and anticipate problems to reduce the potential risk of customer loss.

Salespeople Should Not Ignore Any Customer Problems

It is easy for salespeople to ignore minor customer problems, but the above findings indicate that when salespeople do, there is a 54 to 81% risk that they will lose the customer to a competitor.

More significantly, even when customer problems are resolved, there is a 30 to 46% risk of customer loss, depending upon the degree of the problem.

Salespeople Must Respond Quickly

The most significant finding and best protection against customer loss is the speed with which a problem is responded to and how quickly it is rectified to the customer's satisfaction. When salespeople and their companies respond quickly, the risk of customer loss drops significantly to between 5 and 18%.

Most customers understand that problems will occur, but they expect the salesperson to fix them quickly, fairly, and to their satisfaction. When this is the case, additional surveys have shown that these customers will often turn into the strongest supporters and advocates of the salesperson and his or her company.

POINTS TO PONDER — SOMETHING TO THINK ABOUT

1. Were you surprised by how much of your customer base is at risk?

2. Do these findings personally motivate you to change your attitudes toward and appreciation of your existing customers?

▨ TRAINING ACTIVITY — APPLICATION & ACTION PLAN

1. Based upon the findings listed in this lesson, identify specific strategies and activities to:
   - Pay attention to your customers
   - Deal with any and all customer problems
   - Respond quickly to customer problems

2. Identify areas of potential weakness and ways to reduce the risk of losing your customers to the competition.

About the Author

Timothy F. Bednarz, Ph.D. is CEO of the American Management Development Group, Inc. For over 20 years he has researched, designed and authored hundreds of learning and development programs used by Fortune 1000 companies.

He is also the author of *Great! What Makes Leaders Great. What They Did, How They Did It and What You Can Learn from It* (2011).

Speaking Availability

Timothy F. Bednarz, Ph.D. is available for speaking engagements for your next meeting or association event. He can be contacted at 800-654-4935 or by e-mail at timothy.bednarz@majorium.com.

Bulk Sales

Bulk sales of this book or any other titles available from Majorium Business Press. Inquiries can be directed to sales@majorium.com, or by phone at 800-6654-4935.

Quick Order Form

Fax orders: 715-342-1118. Send this form.

Telephone orders: Call 800-654-4935 toll-free. Have your credit card ready.

Email orders: sales@majorium.com

Postal orders: Majorium Business Press, 2025 Main Street, Stevens Point, WI 54481, USA.

Please send the following books:

_____

_____

_____

_____

Please send more FREE information on:

❑Catalog   ❑Speaking/Seminars   ❑Mailing Lists   ❑Consulting

Name: _____

Address: _____

City: _____ State: _____ Zip: _____

Telephone: _____

Email address: _____

Sales tax: Please add 5.5% for products shipped to Wisconsin addresses.

Shipping by air:

United States: $4.00 for first book and $2.00 for each additional product.

International: $9.00 for first book; $5.00 for each additional product (estimate).

Printed in Great Britain
by Amazon.co.uk, Ltd.,
Marston Gate.